TEMPTATION

PUBLISHED BY LIFEWAY PRESS®

NASHVILLE, TENNESSEE

AUTHORS:
Kenny Luck
Todd Wendorff
Stephen Arterburn

EDITORIAL PROJECT LEADER:
Brian Daniel

ART DIRECTOR & DESIGNER:
Christina Kearney

CONTENT EDITOR:
Brian Gass

PRODUCTION EDITOR:
Bethany McShurley

VIDEO DIRECTOR:
Frank Baker

VIDEO EDITOR:
Phil LeBeau

DIRECTOR, LEADERSHIP AND ADULT PUBLISHING
Bret Robbe

MANAGING DIRECTOR, LEADERSHIP AND ADULT PUBLISHING
Ron Keck

Temptation: Standing Strong Against Temptation

Workbook

Published by LifeWay Press®

©2012 Kenny Luck and Todd Wendorff

Published by arrangement with The WaterBrook Multnomah Publishing Group, a division of Random House, Inc.

ISBN: 978-1-4158-7188-1

Item: 005469695

Dewey Decimal Classification: 248.842

Subject Headings: TEMPTATION\ BIBLE N.T. JAMES STUDY\MEN

Unless otherwise noted, Scripture quotations are taken from the Holman Christian Standard Bible®, Copyright 1999, 2000, 2002, 2003 by Holman Bible Publishers. Used by permission. Scripture quotations marked NASB are taken from the New American Standard Bible®, Copyright © 1960, 1962, 1963, 1968, 1971, 1972, 1973, 1975, 1977, 1995 by the Lockman Foundation. Used by permission. Scripture quotations marked NIV are from the Holy Bible, New International Version, copyright © 1973, 1978, 1984 by International Bible Society.

To order additional copies of this resource,
order online at www.lifeway.com;
write LifeWay Men: One LifeWay Plaza,
Nashville, TN 37234-0175;
fax order to (615) 251-5933; call toll-free (800) 458-2772.

Printed in the United States of America

Leadership and Adult Publishing
LifeWay Church Resources
One LifeWay Plaza
Nashville, TN 37234-0175

Contents

How to Use This Study Guide

Welcome to an eight-week journey into overcoming temptation. Before you get started, here is some helpful information about the different elements you'll encounter within the study:

KEY VERSES AND GOALS FOR GROWTH // Review these items as you prepare for each group meeting. They reveal the focus of the study for the week, will be referenced in Kenny's video message, and will be used in the Connect with the Word personal study time.

INTRODUCTION // This is designed to introduce your study for the week. You will want to read this before your group meets so you'll better understand the topic and the context for your time together.

PERSONAL TIME: CONNECT WITH THE WORD // Complete the Connect with the Word section before each small-group meeting. Consider this section your personal Bible study for the week.

GROUP TIME: REVIEW // The first question in this section is designed to provide you with an opportunity to talk about what God has been revealing to you in your personal time with Him during the past week. The second question is an icebreaker to help you ease into the study topic.

GROUP TIME: VIDEO TEACHING // This listening guide gives you an opportunity to fill in the blanks on important points as you view the video message from Kenny.

GROUP TIME: VIDEO FEEDBACK // This section is designed to facilitate follow-up discussion regarding what you heard from the video message and how you were effected.

GROUP TIME: CONNECT WITH THE GROUP // This portion of your weekly meeting will give you an opportunity to connect with the other men in your group by discussing truths from the Scriptures and the topic for the week and encouraging one another.

WRAP // This section serves as a conclusion to the group time and summarizes key points from your group meeting each week.

Can You Relate?

All men are tempted to compromise their integrity by yielding to unhealthy passions and desires. Yet not all men do. Some have learned the secret of living with undivided thoughts and actions reflecting beliefs. They know how to face temptation without giving in. Every man is tempted to:
- fold when hard times come;
- have an undisciplined thought life;
- give in to sexual temptation;
- fudge on issues of obedience;
- compare himself with and judge others;
- let loose with his tongue in anger;
- buy the lies of materialism; and
- live in isolation from other men.

Dealing with these temptations is a matter of survival. No man can venture into a field of mines without taking precautions. Every God's man must know where the mines are located and learn how to diffuse them.

Our goal in this study is to stimulate personal reflection and honest dialogue. As you work through each session, look at your own life and ask yourself some hard questions. Complete honesty with yourself, with God, and with others will produce the best results.

In the sessions that follow, you will learn to deal with temptation in God's wisdom and strength. By taking God at His Word and applying what He says to your life, you will experience the benefits of an undivided commitment to Christ. You'll find you can live a life of integrity and deal with temptation in a God-honoring way.

Spiritual Integrity

"Surviving the Storms"

A man who survives the trials of life can in time become a man of great character. In fact, character grows strong during times of trial—especially when we choose to hang tough. No man likes trials. We don't go looking for them. We endure them because we have to, not because we want to. But while the hard times tempt us to fold or to try to escape, to give in and grow bitter, perseverance and prayer within our trials inevitably develop our character.

goals for growth

☐ Recognize that God allows trials in our lives to build character.

☐ Understand how to stand strong in the midst of trials.

☐ Commit to praying instead of complaining when faced with trials.

KEY VERSES

2 Consider it all joy, my brethren, when you encounter various trials, 3 knowing that the testing of your faith produces endurance. 4 And let endurance have its perfect result, so that you may be perfect and complete, lacking in nothing. 5 But if any of you lacks wisdom, let him ask of God, who gives to all generously and without reproach, and it will be given to him. 6 But he must ask in faith without any doubting, for the one who doubts is like the surf of the sea, driven and tossed by the wind. 7 For that man ought not to expect that he will receive anything from the Lord, 8 being a double-minded man, unstable in all his ways. 9 But the brother of humble circumstances is to glory in his high position; 10 and the rich man is to glory in his humiliation, because like flowering grass he will pass away. 11 For the sun rises with a scorching wind and withers the grass; and its flower falls off and the beauty of its appearance is destroyed; so too the rich man in the midst of his pursuits will fade away. 12 Blessed is a man who perseveres under trial; for once he has been approved, he will receive the crown of life which the Lord has promised to those who love Him.

(James 1:2-12, NASB)

NOTES

CONNECT WITH THE WORD

THIS SECTION IS DESIGNED TO BE A PERSONAL BIBLE STUDY
EXPERIENCE FOR YOU TO COMPLETE BEFORE YOUR SMALL-GROUP
SESSION EACH WEEK. COME TO YOUR GROUP MEETING PREPARED
TO SHARE YOUR RESPONSES AND PERSONAL APPLICATIONS. YOU
MAY WANT TO MARK OR HIGHLIGHT ANY QUESTIONS THAT WERE
PARTICULARLY MEANINGFUL TO YOU. BEFORE YOU BEGIN YOUR
STUDY, READ THE SCRIPTURES ON PAGE 8.

1. To what kinds of trials do you think James refers in this passage? Why do you think he exhorts us to respond joyfully during
times of trial or testing?

2. Describe how a joyful heart might help you in a difficult time.
(Consider drawing a picture to illustrate.)

3. How does tested faith produce endurance? Describe a time in
your life when you saw this truth at work.

4. How does responding to life's trials with a bad attitude, a complaining spirit, or by running from the situation equal a failure?
Explain.

5. The word endure means "to hold out against." What makes it possible to hold out against—or endure—a trial? Think of a trial you've faced or are facing. What helps you hold out against it in a godly way?

6. According to verse 4, what is the purpose of joyfully enduring a trial to its end?

7. For what should you pray in the midst of a trial (v. 5)? How might this help you overcome a hard situation?

8. In verses 9-11, James contrasts humility (poverty) with pride (riches). How does remaining humble in the midst of a trial help you discover God's purpose for you in it? How might God later use the experience?

REVIEW

What are your expectations of this study?

What about learning to overcome temptation most appeals to you? What difference do you hope it will make in your life?

VIDEO TEACHING

BELOW YOU WILL FIND A LISTENING GUIDE THAT GIVES YOU AN OPPORTUNITY TO FOLLOW IMPORTANT POINTS AS YOU VIEW THE MESSAGE FROM KENNY. WE'LL UNPACK THIS INFORMATION TOGETHER AFTER THE VIDEO.

Watch video session 1: "Surviving the Storms" (9:49).

Pressure is to _TEMPTATION_ what oxygen is to _BREATHING_.

God wants you to use the pressure for _PROGRESS_

God is _PUTTING_ the missing pieces of your _CHARACTER_ in place through pressure.

God's _PURPOSE_ for you is in the pressures you experience.

IF YOU MISSED THIS WEEK'S VIDEO VISIT LIFEWAY.COM/TEMPTATION TO GET CAUGHT UP.

VIDEO FEEDBACK

Kenny contrasts the way the Enemy wants to use pressure in our lives with the outcome that God desires pressure to have. Explain the difference.

Share about a time in your life when you felt pressured and didn't respond to it well. How could you have acted differently? What can we do to instead—as Kenny suggests—get excited about life's pressures?

CONNECT WITH THE GROUP

When Frank Brinner married his sweetheart, Patsy, he didn't have a clue that life would turn out the way it did. Early in their marriage, he enjoyed a successful career, two sons, and a vibrant faith in Christ. Who could ask for more?

Yet shortly into their marriage, the Brinners received the most devastating news of their lives. Patsy was diagnosed with multiple sclerosis, and it would change things forever. Since that day twenty years ago, Frank has cared for his wife's needs on a daily basis. As her health has deteriorated, his care for her has become increasingly painstaking and emotionally draining.

Recently Frank talked with an old friend about a conversation he'd had with his wife. Jokingly Frank had told Patsy, "Honey, I've taken such good care of you that I have all the gray hair. You have none." They laughed together.

That exchange illustrates the upbeat, loving, sacrificial, and joy-filled attitude that has marked the past two decades of Frank's life. Refusing to grow bitter and miserable, he has chosen to deal with his trial joyfully. No man would ask for a trial like that. But sometimes such challenges come whether we like them or not. We don't get to choose our trials, but we do get to choose our responses to them.

1. In what ways can you relate to a trial like Frank's? How do you typically respond when faced with a daunting challenge?

2. What are some harmful ways you have seen men respond to difficult personal situations?

3. What's the difference between enduring a trial and experiencing joy in a trial? How do you think joy enables us to endure?

4. What do you think is the basis of our joy?

Knowledge of who we are in Christ and knowing just what the Enemy is up to help us to confront trials with the right attitude.

5. According to James 1:2-4, what bottom-line benefits do we experience when we rejoice in our trials?

6. What do you think James expects us to do in order to stand under a trial that seems overwhelming?

The pressure that comes with temptation certainly puts us in a place where we must make a decision to either cave in or stand strong. Let's consider the possible spiritual outcomes of dealing with temptation.

7. During times of testing, how is "double-mindedness" revealed in our prayers?

8. In verses 9-12, James described being rich materially but poor spiritually. How do you think trials might help reverse this condition in a man's life?

9. What kinds of trials might the men in your group experience? In what practical ways might you help one another?

WRAP

The Bible is clear: Your hardships are the Lord's instruments; He'll use them to make you into the best God's man you can be. It is never God's will for you to run from your pressures. So be God's man and lean into the pressure that the world brings.

Remember these key thoughts from this week's study:
- Temptation will occur in every man's life.
- The Enemy wants you to react emotionally to pressure.
- God wants to use temptation's pressure to make you stronger.
- When you embrace the pressure of temptation with the right attitude, God will teach you lessons that will shake the Enemy's kingdom.

PRAY TOGETHER

Mental Integrity

"It All Starts in the Mind"

Thoughts flood our minds every day. What we do with them determines who we become.

Extramarital affairs don't happen overnight. (Ask any man who's been through one.) Instead, they brew in a man's mind for weeks and months, even years. When thoughts are allowed to linger on a person or object for any length of time, desire naturally follows. If we choose to long for God, that's a good thing. Choosing to lust for sex proves deadly.

In this session you will see that sexual temptation always starts with a thought. The mind is a very powerful thing. Someone once said, "Sow a thought, reap an action. Sow an action, reap a habit. Sow a habit, reap a character. Sow a character, reap a destiny."

What you think about is important.

goals for growth

☐ Understand the origin of temptation.

☐ Realize that God isn't the one who tempts you.

☐ Commit to controlling your thought life before it controls you.

KEY VERSES

[13]Let no one say when he is tempted, "I am being tempted by God"; for God cannot be tempted by evil, and He Himself does not tempt anyone. [14]But each one is tempted when he is carried away and enticed by his own lust. (James 1:13-14, NASB)

No temptation has overtaken you except what is common to humanity. God is faithful and He will not allow you to be tempted beyond what you are able, but with the temptation He will also provide a way of escape, so that you are able to bear it. (1 Corinthians 10:13)

[1] In the spring when kings march out to war, David sent Joab with his officers and all Israel. They destroyed the Ammonites and besieged Rabbah, but David remained in Jerusalem. [2] One evening David got up from his bed and strolled around on the roof of the palace. From the roof he saw a woman bathing —a very beautiful woman. [3] So David sent someone to inquire about her, and he reported, "This is Bathsheba, daughter of Eliam and wife of Uriah the Hittite." [4] David sent messengers to get her, and when she came to him, he slept with her. Now she had just been purifying herself from her uncleanness. Afterward, she returned home. [5] The woman conceived and sent word to inform David: "I am pregnant." [6] David sent orders to Joab: "Send me Uriah the Hittite." So Joab sent Uriah to David.

7 When Uriah came to him, David asked how Joab and the troops were doing and how the war was going. 8 Then he said to Uriah, "Go down to your house and wash your feet." So Uriah left the palace, and a gift from the king followed him. 9 But Uriah slept at the door of the palace with all his master's servants; he did not go down to his house. 10 When it was reported to David, "Uriah didn't go home," David questioned Uriah, "Haven't you just come from a journey? Why didn't you go home?" 11 Uriah answered David, "The ark, Israel, and Judah are dwelling in tents, and my master Joab and his soldiers are camping in the open field. How can I enter my house to eat and drink and sleep with my wife? As surely as you live and by your life, I will not do this!" 12 "Stay here today also," David said to Uriah, "and tomorrow I will send you back." So Uriah stayed in Jerusalem that day and the next. 13 Then David invited Uriah to eat and drink with him, and David got him drunk. He went out in the evening to lie down on his cot with his master's servants, but he did not go home. 14 The next morning David wrote a letter to Joab and sent it with Uriah. 15 In the letter he wrote: Put Uriah at the front of the fiercest fighting, then withdraw from him so that he is struck down and dies. (2 Samuel 11:1-15)

CONNECT WITH THE WORD

THIS SECTION IS DESIGNED TO BE A PERSONAL BIBLE STUDY
EXPERIENCE FOR YOU TO COMPLETE BEFORE YOUR SMALL-GROUP
SESSION EACH WEEK. COME TO YOUR GROUP MEETING PREPARED
TO SHARE YOUR RESPONSES AND PERSONAL APPLICATIONS. YOU
MAY WANT TO MARK OR HIGHLIGHT ANY QUESTIONS THAT WERE
PARTICULARLY MEANINGFUL TO YOU. BEFORE YOU BEGIN YOUR
STUDY, READ THE SCRIPTURES ON PAGES 20-21.

1. Do you ever blame God for your struggles with temptation?
Why or why not?

2. Read 1 Corinthians 10:13. Scripture is clear that God will not
allow us to be tempted beyond what we can bear and will help us
escape it, but why do you think God allows temptation into our
lives at all?

3. How does lust "carry away" and "entice"? Describe a time when
you experienced this.

4. How have your thoughts contributed to sexual sin?

5. Read 2 Samuel 11:1-15. What havoc did a stray thought cause King David?

6. Where did his spiral into sin begin?

7. What should David have done between verses 2 and 3 that he didn't do?

REVIEW

Consider your personal time management. What things most tempt you to waste time?

Describe a past temptation you faced. What steps did you take (or wish you had) to avoid wandering down the wrong path?

manage our minds

Love for God & people

VIDEO TEACHING

BELOW YOU WILL FIND A LISTENING GUIDE THAT GIVES YOU AN OPPORTUNITY TO FOLLOW IMPORTANT POINTS AS YOU VIEW THE MESSAGE FROM KENNY. WE'LL UNPACK THIS INFORMATION TOGETHER AFTER THE VIDEO.

Watch video session 2: "Mental Integrity" (9:01).

All of your actions begin with *MENTAL* intentions. —

Your mind is *SATAN* target.

2 Cor 10:5

Your mind will make the *difference* in your life.

We must *Manage* our minds aggressively.

Proverbs 4:23
Matt 5:28

High value
① *mind is made for God*

② *battleground*

Luke 4:
attacks —

③ *mind will make the difference*

IF YOU MISSED THIS WEEK'S VIDEO VISIT LIFEWAY.COM/TEMPTATION TO GET CAUGHT UP.

VIDEO FEEDBACK

Kenny discusses the relationship between our thought lives and our actions. Why do you think he places so much emphasis on a man's thoughts?

2 Corinthians 10:5 tells us to take every thought captive. In which parts of your thought life do you do this successfully? Explain.

CONNECT WITH THE GROUP

It all started with an innocent conversation at work. Chris, a married businessman, never thought he'd end up in a yearlong affair with a woman he thought was just an acquaintance. But on a business trip to Las Vegas, she and Chris danced and then kissed and what started as harmless conversation led to a string of lies, liaisons, and more pain and hurt than God ever intended a marriage to endure.

Satan wants us to believe that we can flirt with, get emotionally attached to, and even touch someone other than our spouse and still not violate our marriage covenant. It all seems so innocent. But it's all so wrong.

Thankfully for Chris, years of brokenness, counseling, forgiveness, and the rebuilding of trust led to the restoration of his marriage and family. He never wants to experience that pain again. He shared, "It was like having to start all over again. I had to go back to square one. The pleasure wasn't worth all the pain."

Consider this warning from Stephen Arterburn and Fred Stoeker in *Every Man's Battle*:

> *For males, impurity of the eyes is sexual foreplay.*
> That's right. Just like stroking an inner thigh or rubbing a breast. Because foreplay is any sexual action that naturally takes us down the road to intercourse. Foreplay ignites passions, rocketing us by stages until we go all the way....
> If you're married, you may be asking, *What does all this have to do with me? My foreplay happens only with my wife.*
> Are you sure? Impurity of the eyes provides definite sexual gratification. Isn't that foreplay? When you see a hot movie scene, is there a twitch below your belt? What are you thinking when you're on the beach and suddenly meet a jaw-dropping beauty in a thong bikini? You gasp while Mission Control drones, "We have ignition!" You have her in bed on the spot, though only in your mind. Or you file away the image and fantasize about her later.[1]

1. Imagine yourself as Chris's best friend. How would you have counseled him at each stage of his fall into sin?

2. Do you agree with Chris's assessment that the pleasure he found in the affair wasn't worth all the pain? Why or why not?

While there can be pleasure in sin for a short season, in the end it will always cost more than a God's man should be willing to pay.

3. Respond to the concept of visual foreplay. Do you agree or disagree with the authors' warning?

4. Read Proverbs 7:6-23 and Hebrews 4:15 aloud. Is temptation a sin? Explain.

It's good to remember that even Jesus was tempted, yet did not sin. He modeled how to have our thought lives under control.

5. With what arguments or excuses do we tend to rationalize our wrong responses to sexual temptation?

6. When do you think men are most vulnerable to sexual sin?

7. What steps can we take to deal effectively with sexual temptation before it leads to sin?

8. What can we do this week as a group to help one another in our struggles with sexual temptation?

WRAP

Unfortunately, sexual temptation is a constant threat to our well-being. Like a dangerously sharp rock submerged beneath the surface of the water, lust can potentially rip a huge gash in our hulls and cause us to sink to the bottom should we refuse to steer away from it. The frightening thing is that many men believe themselves immune to the kind of disaster sexual compromise can bring: "It's just a thought. I'm not hurting anyone." But God's man must see temptation as the threat that it is and follow God's plan for overcoming it.

Remember these key thoughts from this week's study:
- Temptation begins in our thoughts.
- The Enemy plans temptation for evil; God uses it for good.
- You must control your thought life or it will control you.

PRAY TOGETHER

1. Stephen Arterburn, and Fred Stoeker. *Every Man's Battle* (Colorado Springs: Waterbrook Press, 2000), 66-67.

Sexual Integrity

"The Other Woman"

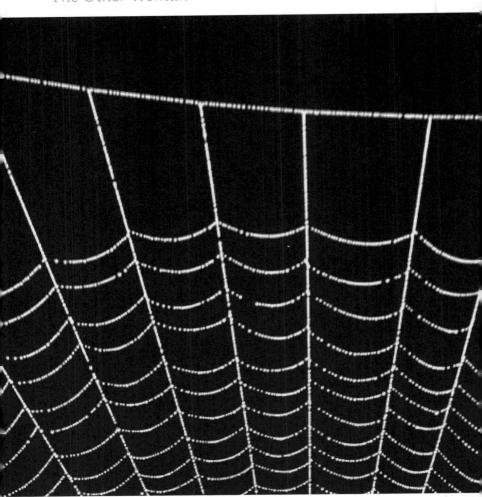

It's one thing to have a lustful thought; it's another to act on it. You know the difference. You are sitting in church, and as you look at a woman nearby, the thought crosses your mind, *That woman has more than a nice outfit.* What we do with our thoughts at times like these will either lead us to victory over sin or increase our vulnerability to it. Sure, you may not act on your thought at that very moment, but if you dwell on it—and keep coming back to it—you will become increasingly vulnerable to sin.

Someone once said, "Be careful what you think about. Your thoughts could become actions at any moment." Those are wise words. If a fantasy is allowed to camp out in your mind, you've already given in. And James said it will lead to sin.

goals for growth

☐ Understand that wrongful actions lead to sin's entanglements.

☐ Become fully aware of the consequences of giving in to temptation.

☐ Acknowledge and accept God's help in standing strong.

KEY VERSES

[15] Then when lust has conceived, it gives birth to sin; and when sin is accomplished, it brings forth death. [16] Do not be deceived, my beloved brethren. [17] Every good thing given and every perfect gift is from above, coming down from the Father of lights, with whom there is no variation or shifting shadow. [18] In the exercise of His will He brought us forth by the word of truth, so that we would be a kind of first fruits among His creatures. (James 1:15-18, NASB)

[21] She seduces him with her persistent pleading; she lures with her flattering talk. [22] He follows her impulsively like an ox going to the slaughter, like a deer bounding toward a trap [23] until an arrow pierces its liver, like a bird darting into a snare—he doesn't know it will cost him his life. (Proverbs 7:21-23)

[1] Now Joseph had been taken to Egypt. An Egyptian named Potiphar, an officer of Pharaoh and the captain of the guard, bought him from the Ishmaelites who had brought him there. [2] The Lord was with Joseph,and he became a successful man, serving in the household of his Egyptian master. [3] When his master saw that the Lord was with him and that the Lord made everything he did successful, [4] Joseph found favor in his master's sight and became his personal attendant. Potiphar also put him in charge of his household and placed all that he owned under his authority.[5] From the time that he put him in charge of his household and of all that he owned, the Lord blessed the Egyptian's house because of Joseph.The Lord's blessing was on all that he owned, in his house and in his fields.

⁶ *He left all that he owned under Joseph's authority; he did not concern himself with anything except the food he ate. Now Joseph was well-built and handsome.* ⁷ *After some time his master's wife looked longingly at Joseph and said, "Sleep with me."* ⁸ *But he refused. "Look," he said to his master's wife, "with me here my master does not concern himself with anything in his house, and he has put all that he owns under my authority.* ⁹ *No one in this house is greater than I am. He has withheld nothing from me except you, because you are his wife. So how could I do such a great evil and sin against God?" (Genesis 39:1-9)*

²⁶ *For on account of a harlot one is reduced to a loaf of bread, And an adulteress hunts for the precious life.* ²⁷ *Can a man take fire in his bosom And his clothes not be burned?* ²⁸ *Or can a man walk on hot coals And his feet not be scorched? (Proverbs 6:26-28, NASB)*

¹⁵ *Drink water from your own cistern And fresh water from your own well.* ¹⁶ *Should your springs be dispersed abroad, Streams of water in the streets?* ¹⁷ *Let them be yours alone And not for strangers with you.* ¹⁸ *Let your fountain be blessed, And rejoice in the wife of your youth.* ¹⁹ *As a loving hind and a graceful doe, Let her breasts satisfy you at all times; Be exhilarated always with her love.*
(Proverbs 5:15-19, NASB)

CONNECT WITH THE WORD

THIS SECTION IS DESIGNED TO BE A PERSONAL BIBLE STUDY
EXPERIENCE FOR YOU TO COMPLETE BEFORE YOUR SMALL-GROUP
SESSION EACH WEEK. COME TO YOUR GROUP MEETING PREPARED
TO SHARE YOUR RESPONSES AND PERSONAL APPLICATIONS. YOU
MAY WANT TO MARK OR HIGHLIGHT ANY QUESTIONS THAT WERE
PARTICULARLY MEANINGFUL TO YOU. BEFORE YOU BEGIN YOUR
STUDY, READ THE SCRIPTURES ON PAGES 32-33.

1. According to James 1:15, what similarities do lust and preg-
nancy share?

2. Does sexual sin always result in death? (See Proverbs 7:21-23.)
What kind of death?

3. In what ways are you being deceived by sexual sin? Be honest
with yourself.

4. God doesn't leave you empty-handed in your struggle against
lust. What help does He offer (James 1:17-18)?

5. James describes our worth to God in verse 18. How might our sense of worth help us avoid giving in to sexual temptation?

6. Read Genesis 39:1-9. What did Joseph do to "deserve" the temptation he faced? Are we ever at fault when we're tempted? Explain your answer. (You might also read Proverbs 7:6-23.)

7. Joseph was tempted to have sex with Potiphar's wife, but how did he respond to her advances?

8. What is the cost of giving in to temptation? The benefit of resisting? (See Proverbs 6:26-28; 5:15-19.)

REVIEW

How would you describe your battle against sexual temptation?

Who do you know that seems to have battled sexual temptation like Joseph and won? How does that person inspire you?

VIDEO TEACHING

▶ BELOW YOU WILL FIND A LISTENING GUIDE THAT GIVES YOU AN OPPORTUNITY TO FOLLOW IMPORTANT POINTS AS YOU VIEW THE MESSAGE FROM KENNY. WE'LL UNPACK THIS INFORMATION TOGETHER AFTER THE VIDEO.

Watch video session 3: "Sexual Integrity" (11:03).

If we don't submit to the pain of *discipline*, we will experience the pain of *regret*.

There is no such thing as an *irresistible* temptation.

A good boundary does not allow temptation to be fertilized by adding *desire*.

Good boundaries starve the *wrong* desires and feed the *right* desires.

renewal pressure

IF YOU MISSED THIS WEEK'S VIDEO VISIT LIFEWAY.COM/TEMPTATION TO GET CAUGHT UP.

VIDEO FEEDBACK

In the video, Kenny quoted Oswald Chambers who said, "Impulse must be trained into intuition through discipline." How have you seen this truth illustrated in your life?

Kenny discussed the importance of setting appropriate boundaries so that we can starve the wrong desires and feed the right ones. What boundaries have you established that could perhaps help the other men in your group?

CONNECT WITH THE GROUP

The authors of *Every Man's Battle* elaborate on the issue of sexual impurity as it relates to God's man:

> "Sexual impurity has become rampant in the church because we've ignored the costly work of obedience to God's standards as individuals, asking too often, 'How far can I go and still be called a Christian?' We've crafted an image and may even seem sexually pure while permitting our eyes to play freely when no one is around, avoiding the hard work of being sexually pure.[1]

> "God is waiting for you," they write to Christian men, "but He is not waiting by the altar, hoping you'll drop by and talk for a while. He is waiting for you to rise up and engage in the battle. We have power through the Lord to overcome every level of sexual immorality, but if we don't utilize that power, we'll never break free of the habit.[2]

1. Discuss your reactions to the two quotes. With what do you most agree or disagree?

2. Describe an experience that confirms something either quote conveys. How has that experience helped clarify your understanding of what's at stake in the battle for sexual integrity?

Most men don't fully realize the connection between thoughts and actions until it is too late. One look leads to another. One thought leads to another. We start to graze with our eyes, and feel we can feast all day long on mental images without anyone getting hurt. But eventually, James said, lust conceives and gives birth to a tangible sinful action.

3. What lies do you tell yourself that intensify your struggle with sexual sin? How do lies function as traps?

4. What steps should you take to break free?

Winning any battle requires a good plan. Compare your action steps. God's men can help one another achieve victory.

5. How might accountability to another God's man help you consistently win the war against sexual sin? How can we make this accountability work within our own small group?

6. What did you learn from your study of Joseph that will help you avoid sexual sin in the future?

Joseph's reaction to temptation is just one example of many that we find in Scripture. To win the battle against sexual sin we must also stay in the Word.

WRAP

The majority of men caught in sexual addiction did not plan it. In fact, many will tell you their downfall started with one crazy idea—a fact that should be enough to scare every one of us into doing a better job of guarding our thoughts. Fear is a great motivator, but our faith backed by a solid plan will allow us to win the victory for sexual integrity every time.

This week, start building into your life three perimeters of defense against sexual temptation:

1. Refuse to look at things you know will tempt you.
2. Screen your thoughts.
3. Commit to Christ daily.

Remember these key thoughts from this week's study:

- Wrongful thoughts lead to wrongful actions that result in sin's entanglements.
- The consequences for giving in to sexual temptation are grave.
- We need faith and a solid plan if we are to maintain sexual integrity.
- We must acknowledge and accept God's help if we are to stand strong.

PRAY TOGETHER

1. Stephen Arterburn, and Fred Stoeker. *Every Man's Battle* (Colorado Springs: Waterbrook Press, 2000), 58.

2. Ibid., 92.

Biblical Integrity

"In One Ear and Out the Other"

We men can talk a good line; but we love to fudge a little with the truth, often projecting an image of ourselves that is something other than reality. We *say* we have it together ... but do we really?

I know a guy who described himself as captain of the USC football team. Technically, his claim was true. School tradition allowed all graduating seniors to be "captain" for the final game. In reality, however, he was captain for only one game and shared that honor with dozens of others!

It's easy to *say* you are a Christian, but do you *live* like a follower? Do you *truly* belong to Jesus or do you allow others to assume your affiliation with Him is deeper than it really is? Relationship with the Lord comes down to obeying the Word. When Scripture says to do something, we've got to do it. Many, though, struggle to give full obedience to God.

In Matthew 7:24 Jesus said, "Everyone who hears these words of mine and puts them into practice is like a wise man who built his house on the rock" (NIV). This week, we will study what biblical integrity means for a God's man.

goals for growth

☐ Realize that selective obedience is not God's will.

☐ Identify areas of selective obedience in your life.

☐ Experience the freedom and joy of complete loyalty to God's Word.

KEY VERSES

[21] Therefore, putting aside all filthiness and all that remains of wickedness, in humility receive the word implanted, which is able to save your souls. [22] But prove yourselves doers of the word, and not merely hearers who delude themselves. [23] For if anyone is a hearer of the word and not a doer, he is like a man who looks at his natural face in a mirror; [24] for once he has looked at himself and gone away, he has immediately forgotten what kind of person he was. [25] But one who looks intently at the perfect law, the law of liberty, and abides by it, not having become a forgetful hearer but an effectual doer, this man will be blessed in what he does. [26] If anyone thinks himself to be religious, and yet does not bridle his tongue but deceives his own heart, this man's religion is worthless. [27] Pure and undefiled religion in the sight of our God and Father is this: to visit orphans and widows in their distress, and to keep oneself unstained by the world.
(James 1:21-27, NASB)

NOTES

CONNECT WITH THE WORD

THIS SECTION IS DESIGNED TO BE A PERSONAL BIBLE STUDY
EXPERIENCE FOR YOU TO COMPLETE BEFORE YOUR SMALL-GROUP
SESSION EACH WEEK. COME TO YOUR GROUP MEETING PREPARED
TO SHARE YOUR RESPONSES AND PERSONAL APPLICATIONS. YOU
MAY WANT TO MARK OR HIGHLIGHT ANY QUESTIONS THAT WERE
PARTICULARLY MEANINGFUL TO YOU. BEFORE YOU BEGIN YOUR
STUDY, READ THE SCRIPTURES ON PAGE 44.

1. According to verse 21, what gets in the way of obedience?

pride, the ways of the world.

2. What might you do to maintain a humble attitude that will-
ingly receives instruction from the Lord?

3. What are some practical differences between doers of the Word
and hearers of the Word?

4. What benefits does a doer of the Word enjoy (v. 25)?

blessed in all that he does.

5. In what ways are you like the man described in verse 25?

6. What proofs of true religion are described in verses 26 and 27? What steps can you take to become more obedient in these areas?

Visit orphans + widows in their distress

Keep oneself unstained by the world.

REVIEW

What did you learn from James 1:25 about a man who actively obeys the Word? In what ways were you able to identify with him?

In what areas do you need to set goals for obedience to Christ? What role will the Bible play in helping you meet those goals?

VIDEO TEACHING

BELOW YOU WILL FIND A LISTENING GUIDE THAT GIVES YOU AN OPPORTUNITY TO FOLLOW IMPORTANT POINTS AS YOU VIEW THE MESSAGE FROM KENNY. WE'LL UNPACK THIS INFORMATION TOGETHER AFTER THE VIDEO.

Watch video session 4: "Biblical Integrity" (10:56).

We can respond to God in _____.

We can respond to God in _____

We can respond to God in _____.

God's man _____ what God _____.

We respond to God because of _____ He is and _____ He has done.

IF YOU MISSED THIS WEEK'S VIDEO VISIT LIFEWAY.COM/TEMPTATION TO GET CAUGHT UP.

VIDEO FEEDBACK

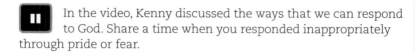 In the video, Kenny discussed the ways that we can respond to God. Share a time when you responded inappropriately through pride or fear.

Describe a time when you chose to respond to God in faith. What difference did it make in your life and in the lives of those in your family or in your church or community?

CONNECT WITH THE GROUP

Why would a California family go to Chicago in March? Well, we all (Todd's family) wanted to see the last snowfall while visiting some good friends. We had to catch a flight home through Denver, and on our way to the gate, I was not impressed with our progress. I was worried that we'd miss our connection unless someone in our party picked up the pace. So I barked out some orders to my wife to "get moving."

Let's just say I failed to accomplish my objective. My wife glared back at me and refused to speed up. When we arrived at the gate in plenty of time to make the flight, I realized immediately that I had a choice to make. Would I rationalize away my sin, or would I admit my wrongdoing and ask for forgiveness?

I decided to take the high road and obey what the Word says. I apologized in front of the kids and half the passengers waiting to board. I'm glad to report that my wife also chose obedience to God's Word: she forgave me.

Often, obedience is the difference between knowing the right thing to do and doing it. And sometimes it will cost you more than a little pride.

1. **What might you have done in Todd's situation?**

2. **What are the three most common ways you selectively obey God's Word?**

3. **Respond to the statement:** *Partial obedience is better than no obedience at all.* **Explain your reaction. How do you think James would respond?**

Both partial and delayed obedience are disobedience to God.

4. What are some practical examples of how partial obedience is accepted by our culture?

5. Why do we tend to hear the Word more than we follow it? What factors create the gap?

6. With which areas of obedience mentioned in verses 26 and 27 do you currently struggle? Give an example.

7. According to verse 26, what is "worthless" religion? How can we, as a group, avoid it?

When our focus is upon religion (the traditions or systems that man puts in place) rather than on our relationship with Christ, we usually miss God's design for our lives.

WRAP

When you know God's standard but rationalize why you don't have to follow it, you'll fool only yourself. Sometimes we allow ourselves to think that we're doing pretty well when it comes to acting on what the Bible commands when in reality we fall short of wholeheartedly living out what God asks of us. We read His Word, but all too often His commands go in one ear and out the other. Unless we obey God in every area of our lives, we fail the ultimate test for biblical integrity.

Remember these key thoughts from this week's study:
- Selective obedience is not God's will for your life.
- We must respond to God in faith rather than pride or fear.
- We respond to God because of who He is and what He has done.
- Freedom and joy come from complete loyalty to God and His Word.

PRAY TOGETHER

Behavioral Integrity

"Judging by Appearances"

When my wife and I (Todd) go out to dinner, I often self-park. (All right, I always self-park.) As we approach the front of the restaurant, it's hard not to notice the $85,000 dark blue Jag, the bright red Porsche, and the silver BMW strategically parked in front of the restaurant.
I bet you've never thought, *So who's the big shot who gets to park in front? I wish I had friends like that!* or *I wish I had money like that!* Oh, the dagger penetrates deep into the flesh…

Comparison is a natural tendency for men. We like to measure a man by his possessions and status. It makes us feel good to find someone lower on the ladder. However, the Bible teaches that net worth does not equal self-worth. Ask James. When we put others down or judge them on the basis of their appearance, status, income, or talent, we become poor judges of character. Comparison spoils our relationships and robs us of the joy of seeing the true worth of others. It also points out our own insecurities and judgmental attitudes.

goals for growth

☐ Learn to treat people fairly.

☐ Grow more sensitive to all people, regardless of their professional status.

☐ Realize that wealth does not make the man.

KEY VERSES

¹ My brethren, do not hold your faith in our glorious Lord Jesus Christ with an attitude of personal favoritism. ² For if a man comes into your assembly with a gold ring and dressed in fine clothes, and there also comes in a poor man in dirty clothes, ³ and you pay special attention to the one who is wearing the fine clothes, and say, "You sit here in a good place," and you say to the poor man, "You stand over there, or sit down by my footstool," ⁴ have you not made distinctions among yourselves, and become judges with evil motives? ⁵ Listen, my beloved brethren: did not God choose the poor of this world to be rich in faith and heirs of the kingdom which He promised to those who love Him? ⁶ But you have dishonored the poor man. Is it not the rich who oppress you and personally drag you into court? ⁷ Do they not blaspheme the fair name by which you have been called? ⁸ If, however, you are fulfilling the royal law according to the Scripture, "YOU SHALL LOVE YOUR NEIGHBOR AS YOURSELF," you are doing well. ⁹ But if you show partiality, you are committing sin and are convicted by the law as transgressors. ¹⁰ For whoever keeps the whole law and yet stumbles in one point, he has become guilty of all. ¹¹ For He who said, "DO NOT COMMIT ADULTERY," also said, "DO NOT COMMIT MURDER." Now if you do not commit adultery, but do commit murder, you have become a transgressor of the law. ¹² So speak and so act as those who are to be judged by the law of liberty. ¹³ For judgment will be merciless to one who has shown no mercy; mercy triumphs over judgment. *(James 2:1-13, NASB)*

¹ The LORD said to Samuel, "How long are you going to mourn for Saul, since I have rejected him as king over Israel? Fill your horn with oil and go. I am sending you to Jesse of Bethlehem because I have

selected a king from his sons." ² Samuel asked, "How can I go? Saul will hear about it and kill me!" The LORD answered, "Take a young cow with you and say, 'I have come to sacrifice to the LORD.' ³ Then invite Jesse to the sacrifice, and I will let you know what you are to do. You are to anoint for Me the one I indicate to you." ⁴ Samuel did what the LORD directed and went to Bethlehem. When the elders of the town met him, they trembled and asked, "Do you come in peace?" ⁵ "In peace," he replied. "I've come to sacrifice to the LORD. Consecrate yourselves and come with me to the sacrifice." Then he consecrated Jesse and his sons and invited them to the sacrifice. ⁶ When they arrived, Samuel saw Eliab and said, "Certainly the LORD's anointed one is here before Him." ⁷ But the LORD said to Samuel, "Do not look at his appearance or his stature, because I have rejected him. Man does not see what the LORD sees, man sees what is visible, but the LORD sees the heart." ⁸ Jesse called Abinadab and presented him to Samuel. "The LORD hasn't chosen this one either," Samuel said. ⁹ Then Jesse presented Shammah, but Samuel said, "The LORD hasn't chosen this one either." ¹⁰ After Jesse presented seven of his sons to him, Samuel told Jesse, "The LORD hasn't chosen any of these." ¹¹ Samuel asked him, "Are these all the sons you have?" "There is still the youngest," he answered, "but right now he's tending the sheep." Samuel told Jesse, "Send for him. We won't sit down to eat until he gets here." ¹² So Jesse sent for him. He had beautiful eyes and a healthy, handsome appearance. Then the LORD said, "Anoint him, for he is the one." ¹³ So Samuel took the horn of oil, anointed him in the presence of his brothers, and the Spirit of the LORD took control of David from that day forward. Then Samuel set out and went to Ramah. (1 Samuel 16:1-13)

CONNECT WITH THE WORD

THIS SECTION IS DESIGNED TO BE A PERSONAL BIBLE STUDY EXPERIENCE FOR YOU TO COMPLETE BEFORE YOUR SMALL-GROUP SESSION EACH WEEK. COME TO YOUR GROUP MEETING PREPARED TO SHARE YOUR RESPONSES AND PERSONAL APPLICATIONS. YOU MAY WANT TO MARK OR HIGHLIGHT ANY QUESTIONS THAT WERE PARTICULARLY MEANINGFUL TO YOU. BEFORE YOU BEGIN YOUR STUDY, READ THE SCRIPTURES ON PAGES 56-57.

1. Why do you think James equated making comparisons with becoming "judges with evil motives" (v. 4)?

2. When are you most tempted to compare yourself with others or judge them? How do you handle this temptation?

3. What does James say in verses 5-7 about the poor and the rich? In light of this passage, how should we view others?

4. Why might James have brought the royal law into the picture in verse 8? (You may also want to refer to Matthew 22:34-40 in your Bible.)

5. According to verse 8, which law sets you free from making comparisons? Why?

6. How should a Christ-follower treat others? When might you need to be especially committed to obedience in this area?

7. Read 1 Samuel 16:1-13. Why do you think Samuel tried to select the next king based on appearance? Describe a time when you made Samuel's mistake. Why is it important that we choose to value a person's heart over his appearance?

REVIEW

Describe a time when you allowed the comparison temptation to lay hold of you. How did you handle the situation?

How have you allowed appearances to distort your judgment? What have you learned from those occasions?

VIDEO TEACHING

▶ BELOW YOU WILL FIND A LISTENING GUIDE THAT GIVES YOU AN OPPORTUNITY TO FOLLOW IMPORTANT POINTS AS YOU VIEW THE MESSAGE FROM KENNY. WE'LL UNPACK THIS INFORMATION TOGETHER AFTER THE VIDEO.

Watch video session 5: "Behavioral Integrity" (12:45).

Men often measure their _____ worth by their net _____.

Material worth is not a real _____ of a man.

Every man wants to be _____ and _____.

Meaning as a man comes from _____ in what God declares to be significant.

God's man focuses on loving _____ and loving _____.

IF YOU MISSED THIS WEEK'S VIDEO VISIT LIFEWAY.COM/TEMPTATION TO GET CAUGHT UP.

VIDEO FEEDBACK

In the video, Kenny talked about the insignificance of our economic accomplishments at our time of death. Describe the end-of-life goals you would like to have in light of this discussion.

Kenny described the injustice of defining other men by their economic status and said it breaks God's heart to see that happen. What can you do to begin to tear down these walls of injustice?

CONNECT WITH THE GROUP

During your discussion time, have in the back of your mind an instance when you totally misjudged someone based on appearances or experienced similar treatment yourself. Consider what emotions might lay behind judgmental thoughts and actions.

1. What harm is there in comparing yourself with others? In judging others? What do these actions say about you?

2. Read Ephesians 6:9 aloud. Applied more broadly, how does this verse remind us that we sometimes treat others wrongly?

3. Looks often deceive. In what ways does James help us avoid judging others based on appearance?

Imagine what would have happened had Samuel's judgment by appearance been the determining factor in who became king of Israel. We would have missed out on King David, the man after God's own heart!

4. How do you want others to see you? Why?

5. What do you think James meant when he spoke of fulfilling the royal law completely?

Complete is a pretty high standard. It's never helpful when we make excuses for the way we view others. As we walk in the Spirit, we will demonstrate the fruit of the Spirit ... to everyone.

6. Read Romans 12:9-20 aloud. According to this passage, what are some specific ways we should treat others?

7. What can you do to be more merciful in your relationships? Give practical examples.

8. In what situations do you show partiality? What steps will you take this week to avoid being judgmental?

WRAP

It is so tempting to compare ourselves to others professionally and financially—especially in the workplace. Even when we meet another man in a social setting, the first question we ask is, "What do you do for a living?" Before the answer comes out of his mouth, we immediately size him up: *What kind of car does he drive? What kind of clothes does he wear? Where does he live?* All such comparisons lead us to play political games and to lack authenticity in our relationships. We fail to treat others as we'd like to be treated; instead, we interact with them based on their worth to us, not on their worth to God.

As we go into the next week, let's instead apply the royal law of God, loving Him and others even as we love ourselves.

Remember these key thoughts from this week's study:
- God's men must learn to treat people fairly.
- We should see people through God's eyes, not our distorted human lenses.
- We are far more than our economic means or social status.
- Keep the Great Commandment: love God and love others as yourself.

PRAY TOGETHER

Verbal Integrity

"Loose Lips"

You said something you didn't mean to say. You wish you could take the words back, but you can't. The worst part is that the person who heard you say that hurtful thing won't ever forget what came out of your mouth.

Did you know that the tongue is the fastest healing body part? Unfortunately, the damage it can cause is not only slow to heal but can last a lifetime. Words are like toothpaste. Once they come out, they can't be stuffed back in. The tongue gets us into trouble more often than any other part of our anatomy. It's just too easy to speak without thinking.

The Bible teaches that we'll either use our words to build others up or to tear them down as we constantly face the temptation to lift ourselves up by verbally attacking others. The tyranny of the tongue lights fires we can't extinguish.

goals for growth

☐ Learn to think before you speak.

☐ Understand the power of your words.

☐ Speak words that build up rather than tear down.

KEY VERSES

[1] Not many of you should become teachers, my fellow believers, because you know that we who teach will be judged more strictly.
[2] We all stumble in many ways. Anyone who is never at fault in what they say is perfect, able to keep their whole body in check. [3] When we put bits into the mouths of horses to make them obey us, we can turn the whole animal. [4] Or take ships as an example. Although they are so large and are driven by strong winds, they are steered by a very small rudder wherever the pilot wants to go. [5] Likewise, the tongue is a small part of the body, but it makes great boasts. Consider what a great forest is set on fire by a small spark. [6] The tongue also is a fire, a world of evil among the parts of the body. It corrupts the whole body, sets the whole course of one's life on fire, and is itself set on fire by hell. [7] All kinds of animals, birds, reptiles and sea creatures are being tamed and have been tamed by mankind, [8] but no human being can tame the tongue. It is a restless evil, full of deadly poison. [9] With the tongue we praise our Lord and Father, and with it we curse human beings, who have been made in God's likeness. [10] Out of the same mouth come praise and cursing. My brothers and sisters, this should not be. [11] Can both fresh water and salt water flow from the same spring? [12] My brothers and sisters, can a fig tree bear olives, or a grapevine bear figs? Neither can a salt spring produce fresh water.
(James 3:1-12, NIV)

When there are many words, sin is unavoidable, but the one who controls his lips is wise. *(Proverbs 10:19)*

Anxiety in a man's heart weighs it down, but a good word cheers it up. *(Proverbs 12:25)*

A hot-tempered man stirs up conflict, but a man slow to anger calms strife. *(Proverbs 15:18)*

Pleasant words are a honeycomb: sweet to the taste and health to the body. *(Proverbs 16:24)*

[27] The intelligent person restrains his words, and one who keeps a cool head is a man of understanding. [28] Even a fool is considered wise when he keeps silent, discerning when he seals his lips. *(Proverbs 17:27-28)*

A man who does not control his temper is like a city whose wall is broken down. *(Proverbs 25:28)*

The mouth speaks from the overflow of the heart. *(Matthew 12:34)*

CONNECT WITH THE WORD

THIS SECTION IS DESIGNED TO BE A PERSONAL BIBLE STUDY EXPERIENCE FOR YOU TO COMPLETE BEFORE YOUR SMALL-GROUP SESSION EACH WEEK. COME TO YOUR GROUP MEETING PREPARED TO SHARE YOUR RESPONSES AND PERSONAL APPLICATIONS. YOU MAY WANT TO MARK OR HIGHLIGHT ANY QUESTIONS THAT WERE PARTICULARLY MEANINGFUL TO YOU. BEFORE YOU BEGIN YOUR STUDY, READ THE SCRIPTURES ON PAGES 68-69.

1. How does the tongue control the whole body?

2. What similarities did James see between the tongue and the rudder of a ship (v. 4)?

3. In what way is an improper word or statement like a lit match in a dry forest? Share an example from your life.

4. What are some practical steps you could take to tame your tongue this week?

5. What can you learn about the tongue from the following Scriptures? Write one truth you learn from each passage.

Proverbs 10:19

Proverbs 12:25

Proverbs 15:18

Proverbs 16:24

Proverbs 17:27-28

Proverbs 25:11

Proverbs 25:28

Matthew 12:34

6. We choose whether to use our mouths to curse or to bless. What are some ways you might bless others with your words?

7. Read James 1:19-20. How do you think angry words block the production of righteousness in us?

REVIEW

Share some of the truths you learned about the tongue from the Bible passages you read.

Describe a time when your tongue got you in trouble. How do you wish you had used it differently?

VIDEO TEACHING

BELOW YOU WILL FIND A LISTENING GUIDE THAT GIVES YOU AN OPPORTUNITY TO FOLLOW IMPORTANT POINTS AS YOU VIEW THE MESSAGE FROM KENNY. WE'LL UNPACK THIS INFORMATION TOGETHER AFTER THE VIDEO.

Watch video session 6: "Verbal Integrity" (13:36).

_____ men will not be _____ encouragers.

A war is raging to stop _____ from flowing from you to other people in your life.

Encouragement is the _____ of every believer's life.

Give away the _____ encouragement that God has given you.

IF YOU MISSED THIS WEEK'S VIDEO VISIT LIFEWAY.COM/TEMPTATION TO GET CAUGHT UP.

VIDEO FEEDBACK

In the video, Kenny differentiates between how we often use our tongues among those closest to us compared to how we use them with those outside our immediate circles. Why do you think we have this tendency? Whom do you hurt the most verbally? What causes you to realize you've spoken harshly?

Read Hebrews 3:12-13. What does this passage teach us about encouragement? Share an example of when you have seen the truth of this passage.

CONNECT WITH THE GROUP

My (Todd's) daughter, Brooke, is an excellent soccer player. Since she doesn't have the height of the other team members, she has to compensate with speed and aggressive play.

During one of her games, she was told to guard Number 8—the opponents' "scoring machine"—with her life. The coach yelled, "Brooke, stay on her. Wherever she goes, you go. Whatever you do, don't let her score."

Brooke went for it and rubbed shoulders with this girl every time she got the ball. After the game she told me that Number 8 yelled at her, "If you touch me again, I'm going to push you to the ground."

Brooke's reponse? "I'm not here to trade insults. I'm here to play soccer."

I can't tell you how proud that made me. Who taught her to say that? Probably her mother, because I would have gone for the jugular. Even though she wanted to return fire, she held her tongue. After the game, Number 8 apologized to Brooke for her threats and words.

How do you respond when ambushed by life? Do you respond in anger? Or, like Brooke, do you consider your response first?

1. We've all said things we later regretted. Share with the group about an experience you've had when you lost control of your tongue.

2. In what situations are you most likely to let loose with angry words? Why?

The tongue reveals to us the depth of our character, and we can't dare to tame the tongue until we've first asked God to fix our hearts.

3. Which word picture about the tongue in James 3:1-12 had the strongest impact on you? Explain.

4. What did you learn from your study of the passages in Proverbs and Matthew? Summarize for the group.

Scripture reminds us about the tongue's power to build up and to destroy. Thankfully, the One who made the tongue lives inside us and has power over it.

5. What can we do to clean up our speech and speak only blessings instead of curses?

6. What relationship(s) in your life will benefit most from your tamed tongue?

7. Using the following chart, take inventory of your words. Commit to speaking words this week that will build others up rather than tear them down.

Words I Say That Destroy	Words I Say That Build Up

WRAP

The tongue is indeed a powerful tool that will produce either good or evil. For many the issue of verbal integrity requires serious application. To whom, if anyone, do you need to apologize for words you spoke in anger? Whom should you build up in Christ's love this week? Share the results with your group during the next session.

Remember these key thoughts from this week's study:
- We must learn to think before we speak.
- We should understand the power of our words. They will either build up or destroy.
- Encouraging should be as natural to us as breathing.
- Ask God for help and practice until verbal integrity is a habit!

PRAY TOGETHER

Moral Integrity

We love toys, don't we? I (Todd) have an awesome mountain bike with full suspension that can climb almost vertical inclines. (Okay, the bike may be able to handle verticals, but I can't.) The point is, it's a really great bike.

But—believe it or not—even though I have such a great bike, I want another one. So, why am I not satisfied with the one I have? Kenny went bike shopping after I got mine, and he one-upped me. You see, I got the Trek Fuel 90; Kenny bought the Trek Fuel 98, which is just a little lighter, a little more versatile—and more expensive. When does this bike envy end?

What's the problem with desiring more? James compared worldliness to committing adultery against God. When we befriend the world, we are committing spiritual adultery! We are being unfaithful to God! It's that serious. Just like a wife who knows when her husband is being overly friendly with another woman, God's Spirit is grieved when our hearts' affections turn away from Him toward pleasures, possessions, and power. We need to end the affair—ASAP.

goals for growth

☐ Identify worldly tendencies in your life.

☐ Understand the destructive nature of materialism.

☐ Learn the remedy for a pride-filled life marked by worldliness.

KEY VERSES

[1] What is the source of wars and fights among you? Don't they come from the cravings that are at war within you? [2] You desire and do not have. You murder and covet and cannot obtain. You fight and war. You do not have because you do not ask. [3] You ask and don't receive because you ask with wrong motives, so that you may spend it on your evil desires. [4] Adulteresses! Don't you know that friendship with the world is hostility toward God? So whoever wants to be the world's friend becomes God's enemy. [5] Or do you think it's without reason the Scripture says that the Spirit who lives in us yearns jealously? [6] But He gives greater grace. Therefore He says: God resists the proud, but gives grace to the humble. [7] Therefore, submit to God. But resist the Devil, and he will flee from you. [8] Draw near to God, and He will draw near to you. Cleanse your hands, sinners, and purify your hearts, double-minded people! [9] Be miserable and mourn and weep. Your laughter must change to mourning and your joy to sorrow. [10] Humble yourselves before the Lord, and He will exalt you. [11] Don't criticize one another, brothers. He who criticizes a brother or judges his brother criticizes the law and judges the law. But if you judge the law, you are not a doer of the law but a judge. [12] There is one lawgiver and judge who is able to save and to destroy. But who are you to judge your neighbor?

[13] Come now, you who say, "Today or tomorrow we will travel to such and such a city and spend a year there and do business and make a profit." [14] You don't even know what tomorrow will bring—what your life will be! For you are like smoke that appears for a little while, then vanishes. [15] Instead, you should say, "If the Lord wills, we will live and do this or that." [16] But as it is, you boast in your arrogance. All such boasting is evil. [17] So it is a sin for the person who knows to do what is good and doesn't do it. (James 4)

CONNECT WITH THE WORD

THIS SECTION IS DESIGNED TO BE A PERSONAL BIBLE STUDY EXPERIENCE FOR YOU TO COMPLETE BEFORE YOUR SMALL-GROUP SESSION EACH WEEK. COME TO YOUR GROUP MEETING PREPARED TO SHARE YOUR RESPONSES AND PERSONAL APPLICATIONS. YOU MAY WANT TO MARK OR HIGHLIGHT ANY QUESTIONS THAT WERE PARTICULARLY MEANINGFUL TO YOU. BEFORE YOU BEGIN YOUR STUDY, READ THE SCRIPTURES ON PAGES 80-81.

1. To what kind of desires did James refer in verse 1?

2. How do our desires get us into trouble sometimes? Share a personal account of how this has happened in your life.

3. According to this passage, what does friendship with the world look like? How does it look in your life?

4. What practical antidote to worldliness do you find in verses 7-10?

5. What kind of man did James describe in verses 13-17? According to James, what's wrong with his thinking? How should he change his thoughts?

6. How can our determination to be successful lead us down a false path? How have you experienced this?

REVIEW

If you recalled an example of a time when your desires got you into trouble, share it with the group.

Think of a book or film where the main character's desires created most of the story's tension. Summarize for the group.

VIDEO TEACHING

▶ BELOW YOU WILL FIND A LISTENING GUIDE THAT GIVES YOU AN OPPORTUNITY TO FOLLOW IMPORTANT POINTS AS YOU VIEW THE MESSAGE FROM KENNY. WE'LL UNPACK THIS INFORMATION TOGETHER AFTER THE VIDEO.

Watch video session 7 "Moral Integrity" (17:54).

Love of the _____ squeezes out the love of the _____.

The values of broken male culture: _____, _____, and _____.

Every man is looking for an _____ in which he can confidently place his masculinity.

God's man must _____ the world in order to _____ the Lord.

IF YOU MISSED THIS WEEK'S VIDEO VISIT
LIFEWAY.COM/TEMPTATION TO GET CAUGHT UP.

VIDEO FEEDBACK

In the video, Kenny talked about the importance of being involved in a local church. Spend a few minutes discussing what that means for you and your group.

What does God opposing the proud look like? What about God giving grace to the humble? Have you seen that pattern in your life? If so, explain.

CONNECT WITH THE GROUP

Jack is not a man of means, but he feels compelled to live like one. His circumstances call for financial discipline, but his lifestyle has given him an image to keep up. He leases an expensive sports car, shops at the most expensive stores, and provides his wife with any earthly comfort they can imagine.

Jack's circumstances say X but he is spending like Y. His image and his reality simply do not jive. He is driven to maintain appearances at all costs—and that can only mean that the world has gotten to him. He's living in a house of (credit) cards that's destined to collapse. As the mountain of debt reaches greater heights, his faith suffers and his marriage swirls down the toilet.

For what? For the image the world has told him he needs to live up to.[1]

1. Imagine yourself as Jack's best friend. What would you say to him about his obsession with image and material possessions? What first step would you recommend he take to break free?

2. In general, what are the signs of materialism in a man's life? In your own life?

Remaining unaware of the signs of materialism may lead us further down the road to ruin than we would ever want to go. It's important we realize the danger early.

3. Define worldly pleasures in light of this week's Scripture.

4. In what ways have you formed a friendship with the world?

5. What steps does James tell us to take to overcome worldliness and materialism? Explain your personal battle plan against the two and prepare to incorporate things you learn from others.

Failure to develop an awareness of materialism and to prepare a personal battle plan to combat it sets us up to lose when temptation strikes. Focusing on spiritual objectives in our own lives and for our families is key.

6. In James 4:13 the businessman says, "We will go...and make a profit." He is oblivious to the fact that life is uncertain. Why is the businessman's way of thinking wrong? Have you ever shared a similar outlook on life? Explain.

7. In what ways does a materialistic focus impact our relationships? Share a personal example, if you can.

8. Which most tempts you: power, possessions, and pleasure? What specific issues do you face in that area?

WRAP

Sadly, the taste of the good life has created in most of us an unquenchable appetite. It drives the average man to work harder than God intended. Worse, it creates an ever-increasing hunger for things. We want what we don't need, and we fight to get those things in order to impress those we don't even know. We become sidetracked with worthless pursuits. The way for God's man is different. God's man must learn to seek first the kingdom of God.

Remember these key thoughts from this week's study:
- We should learn to identify worldly tendencies in our lives.
- We must understand the destructive nature of materialism.
- God's men must create a personal battle plan for combating worldliness.
- Love of the Father will squeeze out the love of the world.

PRAY TOGETHER

Relational Integrity

"Friendly but Friendless?"

goals for growth

☐ Identify the barriers to male accountability.

☐ Be willing to become accountable to other men.

☐ Learn to confess your sins to another man.

Friendless American males live in isolation from others more commonly than you think. How amazing that we can physically stand a few inches from another man's face, yet remain hundreds of miles away from him in terms of making an emotional connection.

Out of fear of exposure we all live in our own private worlds, thinking we can work out our problems. For years we God's men have projected an image that we have it all together, that we're just fine. This leaves us vulnerable to a dangerous pattern. When sin creeps in—rather than seeking another man's help in standing against it—we cover up our pain and failure and go stealth.

Every Christian will sometimes mess up. The question is, Who's going to bring us back from the edge?

KEY VERSES

[13] Is anyone among you suffering? He should pray. Is anyone cheerful? He should sing praises. [14] Is anyone among you sick? He should call for the elders of the church, and they should pray over him after anointing him with olive oil in the name of the Lord. [15] The prayer of faith will save the sick person, and the Lord will restore him to health; if he has committed sins, he will be forgiven. [16] Therefore, confess your sins to one another and pray for one another, so that you may be healed. The urgent request of a righteous person is very powerful in its effect. [17] Elijah was a man with a nature like ours; yet he prayed earnestly that it would not rain, and for three years and six months it did not rain on the land. [18] Then he prayed again, and the sky gave rain and the land produced its fruit. [19] My brothers, if any among you strays from the truth, and someone turns him back, [20] let him know that whoever turns a sinner from the error of his way will save his life from death and cover a multitude of sins. *(James 5:13-20)*

[11] Don't participate in the fruitless works of darkness, but instead expose them. [12] For it is shameful even to mention what is done by them in secret. [13] Everything exposed by the light is made clear,
[14] for what makes everything clear is light. Therefore it is said:
Get up, sleeper, and rise up from the dead, and the Messiah will shine on you. *(Ephesians 5:11-13)*

NOTES

CONNECT WITH THE WORD

THIS SECTION IS DESIGNED TO BE A PERSONAL BIBLE STUDY
EXPERIENCE FOR YOU TO COMPLETE BEFORE YOUR SMALL-GROUP
SESSION EACH WEEK. COME TO YOUR GROUP MEETING PREPARED
TO SHARE YOUR RESPONSES AND PERSONAL APPLICATIONS. YOU
MAY WANT TO MARK OR HIGHLIGHT ANY QUESTIONS THAT WERE
PARTICULARLY MEANINGFUL TO YOU. BEFORE YOU BEGIN YOUR
STUDY, READ THE SCRIPTURES ON PAGE 92.

1. Why is it the responsibility of the one who is sick or suffering to
call on the elders for prayer? What do you think James is trying to
get us to do?

2. How does praying with another person help us through our
problems? When have you benefited from this?

3. How does unconfessed sin create roadblocks to spiritual
growth? Where do you see such blockages in your life?

4. Why do you think we should confess our sins to one another? What good will it do? (See Ephesians 5:11-13.) Have you ever benefited from confession to another man? Explain. According to verses James 5:16, what is the benefit of confessing our sin?

5. What will God do through you when you take accountability seriously (v. 15-16, 19- 20)?

6. How can we actually turn another person from sin?

7. Why do you think James referred to Elijah in this passage? In what ways does the reference to Elijah strengthen the case for having an accountability partner?

REVIEW

Describe how praying with others has impacted your life. What difference might it make in the future?

What role models for friendship do you have either in cultural expressions like film or music or in reality? Explain what you value most about friendship.

VIDEO TEACHING

BELOW YOU WILL FIND A LISTENING GUIDE THAT GIVES YOU AN OPPORTUNITY TO FOLLOW IMPORTANT POINTS AS YOU VIEW THE MESSAGE FROM KENNY. WE'LL UNPACK THIS INFORMATION TOGETHER AFTER THE VIDEO.

Watch video session 8: "Relational Integrity" (21:08).

God has _____ men to deliver justice.

We must let God and _____ _____ into our journey.

There is a war on for your _____ with other men.

_____ makes you vulnerable to Satan's attack.

Secrets give _____ _____ power in your life.

IF YOU MISSED THIS WEEK'S VIDEO VISIT LIFEWAY.COM/TEMPTATION TO GET CAUGHT UP.

VIDEO FEEDBACK

In the video, Kenny shares that men have the ability to refine one another like iron sharpening iron. What does he mean? Give examples from your life.

Kenny describes Satan's desire to devour God's men. How can we possibly be victorious over such a powerful foe? How can our friends help?

CONNECT WITH THE GROUP

I (Todd) was hardly married five years before a good buddy came up to me and said, "Todd, either you go get help, or I'm going straight to your pastor with this." That got my attention. All right, then, the last thing I needed on my hands was full exposure of a problem that I'd been battling for five years. My marriage! Gee thanks, Matt, ole buddy, friend, traitor, tattletale, bonehead. So I took the initiative and went to marriage counseling with my wife. I never realized how much trouble I was in until I sat in the counselor's office and he said, "Let's start where it hurts."

My wife and I began bawling like babies.

As I look back I realize I might never have gotten there and done the hard work of shoring up my marriage if it hadn't been for my buddy Matt. He saved me from a firestorm. My wife was just hanging on, and I didn't even know it. I'd clearly neglected her emotionally while I was busy going to seminary. The irony of that kills me to this day. How could I have let that happen?

Thanks, Matt. I owe you one.

1. **If possible, describe a time when you were saved from a relational firestorm.**

2. **Why do you think men choose not to open up with one another about their struggles?**

3. **Read Proverbs 28:13. What are the consequences of leading an unconfessed, secretive life?**

Transparency and authenticity are key in overcoming the Evil One and living as God's men.

4. Pastor Rick Warren says, "You are as sick as your secrets." Steve Arterburn adds, "Openness is to healing what secrets are to sickness." In what ways does isolation breed sickness in our souls? Do you think God expects us to heal in isolation? What connection does James 5:13-20 make between sickness and sin?

5. What would life look like if God's men practiced biblical confession? What impact do you think our prayers can have on others who are in trouble?

Pride often stands in the way of a man living with relational integrity. Remember, God humbles the proud and exalts the humble.

6. Read Galatians 6:1-5. When might it be right to "go after" another man caught in sin?

7. Who in your life could you trust with your darkest secrets? Are you willing to ask this friend to hold you accountable? Why or why not?

8. Consider a specific struggle you face. Pray for the wisdom to know in whom you can confide about that situation, then write the name of a man with whom you'll share. Commit to talking with him about your situation the next time you get together.

WRAP

Men, you have to have a male friend for accountability. Men become men in the company of men, not women. James said that there will come a time when you will either suffer, grow sick, or sin. Who will be there for you when that happens?

Think about it. Who in your life notices when you are living on the edge of sin? Who notices when things are not right with you—and then asks you about it? Can you name a friend invaluable to your spiritual well-being?

If you are to have victory over the Enemy, you must live with relational integrity—and that begins with accountability.

Remember these key thoughts from this week's study:
- We must become accountable to other men.
- We need to confess our sins to other men.
- The Enemy wants us isolated; God wants us connected.
- Living with secrets will keep us from being God's men.

PRAY TOGETHER

Group Covenant

As you begin this study, it is important that your group covenant together, agreeing to live out important group values. Once these values are agreed upon, your group will be on its way to experiencing true Christian community. It's very important that your group discuss these values—preferably as you begin this study.

PRIORITY: While in this group, we will give the group meetings priority.

PARTICIPATION: Everyone is encouraged to participate and no one dominates.

RESPECT: Everyone is given the right to his own opinions, and all questions are encouraged and respected.

CONFIDENTIALITY: Anything that is said in our meetings is never repeated outside the meeting without permission.

LIFE CHANGE: We will regularly assess our progress toward applying the "steps" to an amazing life of passionately following Christ.

CARE AND SUPPORT: Permission is given to call upon each other at any time, especially in times of crisis. The group will provide care for every member.

ACCOUNTABILITY: We agree to let the members of our group hold us accountable to commitments we make in whatever loving ways we decide upon. Unsolicited advice giving is not permitted.

EMPTY CHAIR: Our group will work together to fill the empty chair with an unchurched man.

MISSION: We agree as a group to reach out and invite others to join us and to work toward multiplication of our group to form new groups.

MINISTRY: We will encourage one another to volunteer to serve in a ministry and to support missions work by giving financially and/or personally serving.

I, _____, agree to all of the above.
Date: _____

Leader Guide

We hope the information provided on the following pages will better equip you to lead your study of *Temptation: Standing Strong Against Temptation.* In addition to the general notes to help you along the way, we've included the answers for the video listening guides for each session. These may be useful to you if someone misses a session and would like to fill in the blanks.

This study is designed to cover an eight-week time frame. However, it is not unusual for a group to spend two or three meetings completing one lesson. Always go for depth over distance. And don't hesitate to adapt this study so that it truly works for you.

Note: You may consider bringing your men together before your first "official" meeting to pass out member books or just to give them an opportunity to check things out before they commit to the study. This would be a great time to show the Get Healthy Series overview (10:03) to those in attendance so they can get an introduction to the series. You will find this overview on the DVD in your Leader Kit.

SESSION 01_SPIRITUAL INTEGRITY

Key Verses and Goals for Growth—You'll want to review these items as you prepare for each small-group session.

Introduction—Each session begins with a narrative overview of the weekly topic. This material is designed to help you introduce the topic of study. You will want to read this before your group meets so that you'll better understand the topic and the context for your time together. For weeks 2-8, suggest that group members read this before you meet.

Personal Time: Connect with the Word—Each member of your small group should complete this section before the small-group meeting. In order for them to have the opportunity to complete this portion of the study before your week 1 meeting, ask group members to purchase their workbooks in advance or make plans to get them workbooks ahead of time.

Group Time: Review—In weeks 2-8 the first question in this section will be used to talk about what God has been revealing to group members from their time with Him during the week. In this session, however, you'll talk in more broad terms about their expectations and what most appealed to them about this study. These questions are intended to be nonthreatening to group members so that a pattern of participation can be established early on.

Group Time: Video Teaching—Encourage group members to follow along, fill in the blanks on page 13, and take additional notes as they hear things that speak strongly to their own stories.

> Pressure is to <u>temptation</u> what oxygen is to <u>breathing</u>.
> God wants you to use the pressure for <u>progress</u>.
> God is <u>putting</u> the missing pieces of your <u>character</u> in place through pressure.
> God's <u>purpose</u> for you is in the pressures you experience.

Group Time: Video Feedback—This section is designed as follow-up to the video message. You will want to use the listening guide to highlight the main teaching points from the video and process with the group what they heard and how they were affected.

Group Time: Connect with the Group—In Session 01 you will talk as a group about spiritual integrity and its role as the foundation for surviving the storms of life.

Wrap—At this point each week, you will want to close the group time in prayer. You may want to use this time to reflect on and respond to what God has done in your group during the session. Invite group members to share their personal joys and concerns. For this week, it's probably best for you to pray for the group. In coming weeks, as group members get more comfortable, consider asking for volunteers to lead the group in prayer.

SESSION 02_MENTAL INTEGRITY

Introduction—Welcome group members back. Use the narrative overview on page 19 to introduce the topic for Session 02. Make sure you read this before your group meets so that you'll better understand the topic and the context for your time together.

Personal Time: Connect with the Word—Encourage the men to use this as their personal Bible study for the week.

Group Time: Review—This week you will talk about what the Lord has revealed to you over the past week regarding temptation and how stray thoughts play such a key role. Continue to encourage group members to share during this time.

Group Time: Video Teaching—Encourage group members to follow along, fill in the blanks on page 25, and take additional notes as they hear things that speak strongly to their own stories.

> All of your actions begin with <u>mental</u> intentions.
> Your mind is <u>Satan's</u> target.
> Your mind will make the <u>difference</u> in your life.
> We must <u>manage</u> our minds aggressively.

Group Time: Connect with the Group—In Session 02 you will work on recognizing the role that our minds play in taking us further down the road of temptation.

Wrap—This week you may consider asking for a volunteer to lead the group. Ask the Lord for help in renewing your minds so that you may be victorious over temptation.

SESSION 03_SEXUAL INTEGRITY

Introduction—Use the narrative overview on page 31 to introduce the topic of study for Session 03. Read this before your group meets so that you'll better understand the topic and the context.

Personal Time: Connect with the Word—Encourage the men to use this as their personal Bible study for the week.

Group Time: Review—This week you will be talking about what the Lord has revealed to you over the past week regarding sexual sin and the importance of resisting.

Group Time: Video Teaching—Encourage group members to follow along, fill in the blanks on page 37, and take additional notes as they hear things that speak strongly to their own stories.

> If we don't submit to the pain of <u>discipline</u>, we will experience the pain of <u>regret</u>.
> There is no such thing as an <u>irresistible</u> temptation.
> A good boundary does not allow temptation to be fertilized by adding <u>desire</u>.
> Good boundaries starve the <u>wrong</u> desires and feed the <u>right</u> desires.

Group Time: Connect with the Group—You will talk about the importance of guarding against evil desires and feeding desires for kingdom righteousness.

Wrap—Close your group time in prayer, asking God to help you overcome sexual temptation.

SESSION 04_BIBLICAL INTEGRITY

Introduction—Use the narrative overview on page 43 to help you introduce the topic of study for Session 04.

Group Time: Review—This week you will be talking about the need for biblical integrity. In preparation for this week's topic, you'll talk about your steps toward obedience to Christ.

Group Time: Video Teaching—Encourage group members to follow along, fill in the blanks on page 49 and take additional notes as they hear things that speak strongly to their own stories.

We can respond to God in <u>pride</u>.

We can respond to God in <u>fear</u>.

We can respond to God in <u>faith</u>.

God's man <u>does</u> what God <u>wants</u>.

We respond to God because of <u>who</u> He is

and <u>what</u> He has done.

Group Time: Connect with the Group—In Session 04 you will talk about the importance of complete obedience to God's Word—being doers of the Word and not hearers only.

Wrap—Request that a volunteer close your group time in prayer, asking God to help group members faithfully obey Christ.

SESSION 05_BEHAVIORAL INTEGRITY

Introduction—Use the narrative overview on page 55 to help you introduce the topic of study for Session 05.

Group Time: Review—This week you will be talking about what the Lord has revealed to you over the past week regarding the way we view others. In preparation for this week's topic, you'll talk about the ways that you have allowed appearances to distract you from God's view of others.

Group Time: Video Teaching—Encourage group members to follow along, fill in the blanks on page 61, and take additional notes as they hear things that speak strongly to their own stories.

Men often measure their self <u>worth</u> by their net <u>worth</u>.

Material worth is not a real <u>reflection</u> of a man.

Every man wants to be <u>valued</u> and <u>validated</u>.

Meaning as a man comes from <u>investing</u> in what God declares to be <u>significant</u>.

God's man focuses on loving <u>Him</u> and loving <u>others</u>.

Group Time: Connect with the Group—In Session 05 you will learn about keeping God's royal law toward others.

Wrap—Request that a volunteer close your group time in prayer, asking God to help you show mercy to others—even if they don't deserve it.

SESSION 06_VERBAL INTEGRITY

Introduction—Use the narrative overview on page 67 to help you introduce the topic of study for Session 06.

Group Time: Review—This week you will be talking about what the Lord has revealed to you over the past week regarding the way that you use your tongue. In preparation for this week's topic, you'll talk about how you have gotten into trouble by the misuse of your tongue.

Group Time: Video Teaching—Encourage group members to follow along, fill in the blanks on page 73, and take additional notes as they hear things that speak strongly to their own stories.

> Under-encouraged men will not be over-liberal encouragers.
> A war is raging to stop encouragement from flowing from you to other people in your life.
> Encouragement is the oxygen of every believer's life.
> Give away the same encouragement that God has given you.

Group Time: Connect with the Group—In Session 06 you will talk about the importance of not only taming your tongue but using it as an instrument of blessing.

Wrap—Close the group in prayer, thanking God for the gift of encouragement and trusting Him to help you extend it.

SESSION 07_MORAL INTEGRITY

Introduction—Use the narrative overview on page 79 to help you introduce the topic of study for Session 07.

Group Time: Review—This week you will be talking about what the Lord has revealed to you over the past week regarding our desire for the world and the things in it. In preparation for this week's topic, you'll talk about a time when your worldliness got you into trouble.

Group Time: Video Teaching—Encourage group members to follow along, fill in the blanks on page 85, and take additional notes as they hear things that speak strongly to their own stories.

Love of the <u>world</u> squeezes out the love of the <u>Father</u>.
The values of broken male culture: <u>indulge, impress,</u> and <u>increase</u>.
Every man is looking for an <u>identity</u> in which he can confidently place his masculinity.
God's man must <u>defriend</u> the world in order to <u>befriend</u> the Lord.

Group Time: Connect with the Group—In Session 07 you will talk about materialism and the way that it interferes in our relationships with God and others.

Wrap—Close the group in prayer, asking God to keep you mindful of opportunities to avoid materialism by giving to others.

SESSION 08_RELATIONAL INTEGRITY

Introduction—Use the narrative overview on page 91 to help you introduce the topic of study for Session 08.

Group Time: Review—This week you will be talking about what the Lord has revealed to you over the past week regarding accountability. In preparation for this week's topic, you'll talk about how you have seen true friendship modeled.

Group Time: Video Teaching—Encourage group members to follow along, fill in the blanks on page 97, and take additional notes as they hear things that speak strongly to their own stories.

> God has <u>hard-wired</u> men to deliver justice.
> We must let God and <u>other men</u> into our journey.
> There is a war on for your <u>relationships</u> with other men.
> <u>Isolation</u> makes you vulnerable to Satan's attack.
> Secrets give <u>the Devil</u> power in your life.

Group Time: Connect with the Group—In Session 08 you will talk about the importance of confession to others. Also, be sure to discuss next steps with your group and encourage the men to Get In, Get Healthy, Get Strong, and Get Going. Go to LifeWay.com/Men for more help in developing your church's strategy for men.

Wrap—Ask as many group members as will to pray aloud, thanking God for this eight-week journey you have completed together.

If you want true intimacy and connection with a woman, you'll need to grow up and graduate from God's school of character. This "Get Healthy" study is the perfect start.

This "men's ministry in a box" provides everything a church needs to re-boot or initiate a men's ministry. It defines the four pillars of a successful model and also provide solutions for each pillar.

Biblical Solutions for men

Looking for more Kenny Luck resources? Here are the latest from LifeWay. To learn about our new men's ministry strategy, which is based on Kenny Luck's success at Saddleback Church, scan this barcode with your phone's QR code reader.

www.lifeway.com/men | 800.458.2772 | LifeWay Christian Stores

Group Directory

Name: _____
Home Phone: _____
Mobile Phone: _____
E-mail: _____
Social Networks(s): _____

Name: _____
Home Phone: _____
Mobile Phone: _____
E-mail: _____
Social Networks(s): _____

Name: _____
Home Phone: _____
Mobile Phone: _____
E-mail: _____
Social Networks(s): _____

Name: _____
Home Phone: _____
Mobile Phone: _____
E-mail: _____
Social Networks(s): _____

Name: _____
Home Phone: _____
Mobile Phone: _____
E-mail: _____
Social Networks(s): _____

Name: _____
Home Phone: _____
Mobile Phone: _____
E-mail: _____
Social Networks(s): _____

Name: _____
Home Phone: _____
Mobile Phone: _____
E-mail: _____
Social Networks(s): _____

Name: _____
Home Phone: _____
Mobile Phone: _____
E-mail: _____
Social Networks(s): _____

Name: _____
Home Phone: _____
Mobile Phone: _____
E-mail: _____
Social Networks(s): _____

Name: _____
Home Phone: _____
Mobile Phone: _____
E-mail: _____
Social Networks(s): _____

Name: _____
Home Phone: _____
Mobile Phone: _____
E-mail: _____
Social Networks(s): _____

Name: _____
Home Phone: _____
Mobile Phone: _____
E-mail: _____
Social Networks(s): _____

Name: _____
Home Phone: _____
Mobile Phone: _____
E-mail: _____
Social Networks(s): _____

Name: _____
Home Phone: _____
Mobile Phone: _____
E-mail: _____
Social Networks(s): _____